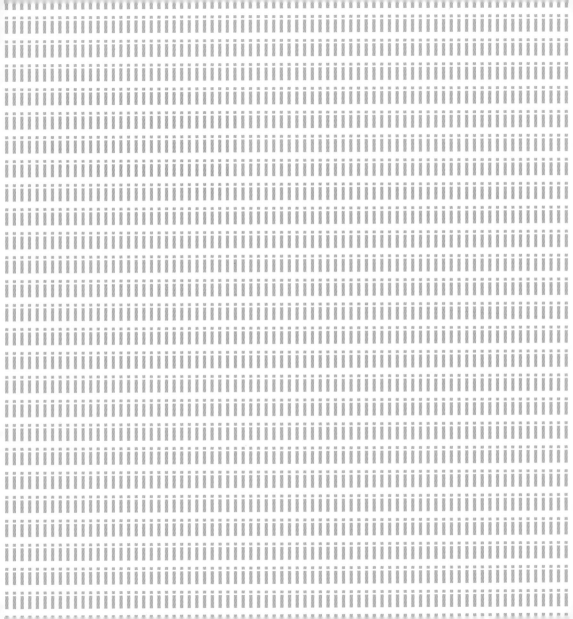

Missing Ingredients
for Team Success

TEAM

THE ^ IN TEAM

simple truths®
Your Destination For Inspiration
an imprint of Sourcebooks, Inc.

John J. Murphy and
Michael McMillan

Editing by: Alice Patenaude
Design and graphics by: Michael McMillan and Megan Kearney

Photo Credits:
Internal: page 5, astudio/Shutterstock; page 29, pashabo/Shutterstock; page 35, Dusan Po/Shutterstock; page 41, Roman Sotola/Shutterstock; page 55, Shutterstock; page 69, skyboysv/Shutterstock

Published by Simple Truths, an imprint of Sourcebooks, Inc.
P.O. Box 4410, Naperville, Illinois 60567-4410
(630) 961-3900
Fax: (630) 961-2168
www.sourcebooks.com

Printed and bound in China.
RRD 10 9 8 7 6 5 4 3 2

Contents

"Do ya see an i?" my high school football coach yelled as he scratched TEAM on the board, breaking the chalk a few times along the way. It was halftime and we were losing. My coach was passionate about winning. More accurately, he hated losing. Hearts pounding, my teammates and I sat silently with our helmets on for protection. With bulging eyes, popping neck veins, and a raspy voice he repeated, "Do any of ya see an i?"

Even if I had seen the i in TEAM back then, I wouldn't have raised my hand. We were a team. And we had no place for individual egos on our team. Of all the sayings, "There's no i in TEAM" was my coach's favorite. The letters on the chalkboard confirmed his claim...hence the clever play on a word.

If you disregard this book's cover and its contents, the "No i" idiom makes sense. If you don't, you'll discover not only is there an i in TEAM— there are many. No i's, no team. No team, no teamwork. Are we proposing the concept behind "There's no i in TEAM" is wrong? No! It's just limited. Members on high-performing teams always put team first. It's what they do in addition that separates them from the competition.

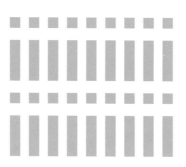

Clearly, I'm the best!

When asked, most people initially see one big i rather than 63 individual i's or 126 shapes. Identifying the "parts" that create the "whole" requires looking beyond the obvious.

Like my coach, some leaders are more passionate about not losing than developing sustainable, winning teams. Fear of failing can temporarily motivate us, but the long-term consequences are destructive on many levels. This negative approach prevents honest interaction and violates trust—key ingredients for synergy to emerge. To build successful teams, leaders must see the full picture and understand how all the parts establish the team and determine its performance.

Edgar Rubin's classic example of figure-ground perception demonstrates our limited perception. Is it two faces or a vase? It's both. Which is most important? Neither the faces nor the vase would exist without the other. While Rubin's example shows why people miss the i in the word TEAM... it also sheds light on why we miss the ingredients required for successful teamwork. For teams to reach full potential, leaders must develop excellent perception skills—the ability to shift between the team and its members. Performance teamwork emerges once a team is significantly greater than the sum of its members—its i's.

As you build your organization's performance, please consider the teams to which we all belong. By rekindling the i in our families, schools, neighborhoods, and societies, we can impact the world in positive ways.

We have been fortunate to work with many high-performing teams around the world. From executive teams in London, Basel, and New York to creative teams in San Francisco, Vancouver, and Chicago to military and defense teams in Boston, Washington, D.C., and San Diego to kaizen teams in Shanghai, Lisbon, and Buenos Aires, one thing is perfectly clear. There is an i in TEAM! In fact, there are many i's in TEAM. They are the very stitching that holds high-performing teams together and makes them unique. They give high-performing teams a competitive edge. They are a differentiator, a strategic advantage. They generate synergy, the power of teamwork.

These essential i's—often hidden from view—are exactly what many low-performing teams are painfully missing. Do not be fooled by superficial rhetoric, catchy slogans, and idealistic assumptions. Subtle as they may be, the i's in team must be identified, understood, honored, and put to good use. These i's in TEAM make all the difference.

In this book, we will reveal these i's. We will challenge the assumption that "There's no i in TEAM." As expressed in Michael's foreword, we understand the concern and positive intent that many people have when they make this statement, but we also understand that it is an i who says it. It is an *individual* sharing an independent idea, a personal point of view. It is simply an input.

We are all individuals and we are all unique. As individuals, we often express independent points of view. We each have our own interpretations of things. Our insights, inspirations, and intuitions give us different perspectives. Our imaginations show us different mental images, pictures, and possibilities. We are all different instruments playing in a sacred, interdependent orchestra. These are differences to be honored and built upon, not criticized or judged. Just because someone doesn't see things our way or agree with us on an option, this does not make them wrong or selfish. In fact, it may be just what we need to hear at the time to think at a deeper level and find more creative, sustainable solutions. We may discover that it is our own clouded filters and uncontrolled judgment that create the problem.

ME
WE

8

Yes, we often find ourselves challenged with "me-opic" conditioning, or "What's in it for me?" The wise team leader understands this and perhaps even expects it. It is indeed what makes the team unique. Like a game of cards, we may all be dealt a different hand. We all have diversity to deal with in one way or another. Sometimes this can most certainly test our patience. Just remember, a royal flush beats four-of-a-kind every time. Both hands are alike and both hands have differences. More often than not, what we see and how we play it rests in the i of the beholder.

OPIC

To perform habitually at peak levels, we have to drill down beneath the superficial level and look at things differently, including ourselves, the world we live in, and the problems we face. Perhaps these problems are exactly what we need at this time to learn, grow, and elevate our game. To truly step up, we have to uncover and challenge the subconscious beliefs and limiting interpretations driving our attitudes and restricting our results. After all, we reap what we sow.

Great teams take time to ask what if, why, and why not. We exercise our intuition, our imagination, and our ingenuity—all critical i's to high-performance teamwork. We learn to suspend judgment and open our minds and our hearts, allowing us to "wake up" and become aware of information and insights we never saw before. In doing so, we gain intelligence, another critical i in teamwork. We experience paradigm shifts, a reprogramming of the habitual mind. We shift from me-opic to we-opic vision, transcending independent thinking and unleashing interdependent power. We let go of insecurity and limiting beliefs and develop trust within the team.

In doing so, we uncover win-win solutions, mutually beneficial results that defy the assumptions of scarcity. There is no better way to do this than through healthy, cooperative teamwork, the very process of challenging one another to find a better way for everyone.

When we work alone, our assumptions go unchecked. We do the best we can with what we know. However, when we work in teams, our assumptions and limiting beliefs are revealed through our expressed attitudes, choices, behaviors, and results. When someone says to us "What are you thinking?" or "Why would you do that?" they are challenging our assumptions, a very important habit among healthy teams. This is not a comment or question to take personally. Consider it a gift, perhaps even a blessing in disguise. It could save the whole team.

Here rises the challenge—and power—of teamwork. We all make assumptions. We have to. In the absence of perfect knowledge and complete factual data, we have to make decisions and choose options with uncertainty. We have to exercise our intuition.

Now what? Do we point the finger at each other and proclaim non-team-play? Do we accuse one another of not understanding there is no i in team? Or do we recognize that there is an i in team and it is the healthy expression of it that, in fact, leads us to synergistic answers and solutions. The i is not our problem. It is our inability to pull it together and make good music with it that is the problem. Our orchestra would be severely limited if we all played the same instrument and only one song.

The purpose of this book is to challenge some common misperceptions about teamwork and provide useful ideas on effective team leadership. To get the most out of this book, let go of any temptations to jump to conclusions, close the mind, or insist on being right. Let go to let flow. Suspend any immediate, habitual judgment and contemplate what we offer. Look for the hidden gems in the dark and rocky soil. Trust the wisdom of the ages. Seek and ye shall find. There are many i's in team.

Use this book to:

- Tap the unique potential, inputs, and talents of the individuals on your team

- Create more intrigue, involvement, and interaction among team members

- Inspire true, high-performance teamwork and synergy

- Cultivate an interdependent, we-opic, and shared vision

- Exercise intuition to develop an environment of imagination, ingenuity, and innovation

- Build team intelligence

- Foster team integrity

- Increase your return on investment

inspi

ration

If you wait around for the clouds to part and a bolt of lightning to strike you in the brain, you are not going to make an awful lot of work. All the best ideas come out of the process; they come out of... the work itself.

—Chuck Close

One of the first things we witness when working with high-performance teams around the world is that there is a tremendous amount of inspiration driving the team. These teams are purposeful and powerful. They want to accomplish something meaningful and significant to all. The vision and mission are clear to everyone. There is no doubt or hesitation holding team members back. Goals are SMART—Specific, Measurable, Attainable, Relevant, Timed. Metrics are in place to track and report what matters. There is context that makes the content meaningful. The team is aligned and informed. The team is practiced and prepared. We are not trapped in the weeds, trying to figure out what to do. We are not winging it. We see clearly. We see as one, with a collective mind and a united spirit. We perform well because we are focused and inspired to perform well. A team without inspiration is a team without energy.

High-performing teams are proactive and assertive. We are positive and optimistic. We know we can do better and we continuously seek ways to do this. There is no room for complacency, negativity, or pessimism on a great team. These toxic assumptions and attitudes must be challenged. Problems must be perceived as solutions in disguise. Crises must be seen as opportunities for growth and contribution. Challenges must be viewed as lessons to be learned.

The spirit and life force within all of us seeks ongoing expansion and growth. It is like a child searching for new meaning and exploring ways to be creative. The problem is that many work environments restrict, and even forbid, this powerful flow of energy. Rather than tapping it through meaningful participation and proactive involvement, the organization limits it. People are simply told to follow procedures and do as they are told. Mindful people are conditioned to be mindless.

We use methods like team kaizen events to unleash creativity and evoke passion and spirit in the workplace. Kaizen is a Japanese word that essentially translates into "good change." When we combine the power of positive, Zen thinking with a proactive approach to change management, we can quickly see the best in people come alive.

A typical kaizen event takes five days, following a three- to four-week preparation period. During the preparation phase, the team applies specific data collection and mapping tools to clearly define the current state with facts. This grounds the team in reality, increases awareness, and builds a sense of urgency. Kaizen is about making change, not talking about it. It is about acting on ideas and innovating, not holding back. This is where we often witness what some people call miracles—shifts in perception and astounding results. Team members who are skeptical on Monday are celebrating with enthusiasm and conviction on Friday. Perceptions have shifted as changes have been made. The mind and the heart are now one—evoking great courage, passion, and determination—as "good change" is implemented and nagging problems resolved. Make no mistake...there is an i in team. It is called inspiration.

interdep

endence

Independent thinking alone is not suited to interdependent reality. Independent people who do not have the maturity to think and act interdependently may be good individual producers, but they won't be good leaders or team players. They're not coming from the paradigm of interdependence necessary to succeed in marriage, family, or organizational reality.

—Stephen R. Covey

One of our favorite exercises in team-building workshops is a simulated "survival" activity. We begin by having participants complete a paper-and-pencil instrument independently, ranking fifteen items in terms of their importance to surviving a crisis event (e.g., a crash landing in unknown territory like a desert, subarctic, or jungle region). The idea of the exercise is to examine how people make decisions, first individually, and then as a team. Once everyone has completed ranking the items independently, we form teams and have them repeat the exercise using an interdependent, consensus process. In both cases, the participants have to select their items based on limited information and assumptions. It becomes quite clear that flawed assumptions can be disastrous in the exercise, just like in real life.

An interesting result of this simulation is that the teams consistently outperform their own average individual scores. In fact, most teams survive (according to a survival expert's well-researched ranking), while most individuals do not. Why is this? What is the secret? It is clearly more than coincidence.

The answer is *interdependent* thinking—how can we help one another help one another? How can I help you help me? Where is the creative, win-win solution?

One of the most powerful creative problem-solving techniques we know is to find at least three options for each problem. It is simply too easy for someone to say, "Don't come to me with a problem without a solution." We all hear this from time to time. The wise leader suggests, "Don't come to me with a problem without at least three solutions!"

Why is this important? Because when we explore additional options with an open mind, new insights appear. We may have originally assumed that option A would be best. By searching for an option B and C, we are forced to think beyond the first "right" answer. This approach also helps teams break free of gridlock and impasse over option A or B. If we can't agree or come to consensus, let's look further. There are always alternatives.

Now the question becomes, which option is best, A, B, or C? When we ask this question in workshops, we regularly get a range of answers from A to C. Let's call these answers "inside the A-C box" options. The better answer is actually option D, an option that was not even considered originally as a choice! Where did option D come from? It came from a team that is now more open and creative in working together interdependently. This powerful team-building technique reminds us that we are better off focusing on common interests and not conflicting positions. Interests tend to unite us (like survival). Positions divide us (and are often based on assumptions). Inter-dependent thinking reminds us to think we-opically and find solutions that are win-win. It does us little good to solve one problem and create more problems in the process. Look carefully at great teams and you will find another i in play. It is called interdependence.

AT A GLANCE

- Interdependence means finding win-win solutions to every problem.
- Interdependence means exercising "we-opic" vision—asking "What's in it for we?"
- Interdependence means putting the team first and generating synergy, the power of teamwork

TEAM EXERCISE

Conduct a workshop with your team using an experiential exercise (like a survival simulation). First, have team members complete the exercise alone, independently. Take note of the various assumptions made. How do these assumptions influence decisions? How do perceptions drive behaviors? Next, have teams of five to seven people complete the exercise. Encourage them to find answers they can all agree on, to reach true consensus. Use audio or video feedback for review if possible. Examine and learn from the results. Discuss the various assumptions made and the impact of interdependent thinking on the team. Help team members see and understand the power of teamwork by experiencing it.

intelli

gence

Talent wins games, but teamwork and
intelligence wins championships.

—Michael Jordan

How effective is a team of highly skilled Navy Seals without accurate intelligence? How successful is a group of gifted athletes without a winning game plan? Can a good team compete and continue to win great victories without clear and competent guidance? The evidence suggests not.

Teams of well-trained people with positive intent lose frequently. It takes more than physical prowess to compete at world-class levels. We need more than recruiting and training to compete like champions. Yes, we need to understand and be inspired by our mission. Yes, we need to think and act interdependently. And yes, we need to be smart. Intelligence plays a key role in differentiating great teams from strong competitors.

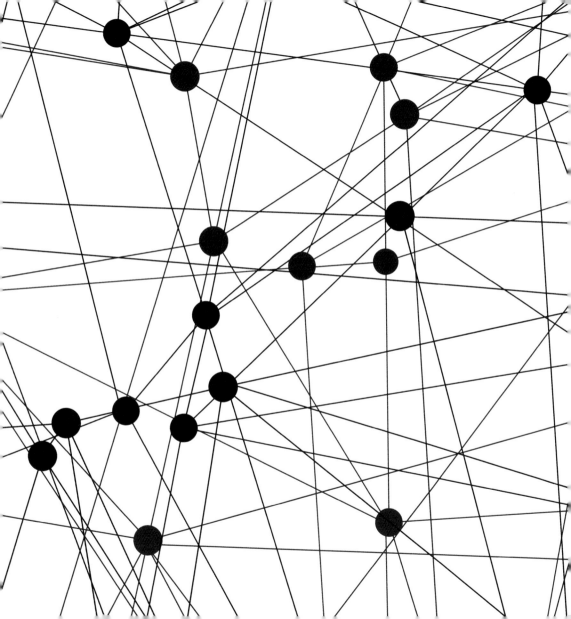

Here are just a few critical intelligence factors to consider:

- We need to understand our customers and our stakeholders—what they value, what they need, and what they don't want.
- We need to understand our playing field—our market and environment.
- We need to understand our competition—any and all forces against us.
- We need to understand our own strengths and weaknesses as a team.
- We need to know our individual players and their capabilities.
- We need to position people where they can add the most value.
- We need to know how to achieve our goals and mitigate risk.
- We need a winning strategy and game plan.

When I (John) was in high school, my football team won the state championship. It was certainly not because we had the best athletes in the state. We had good athletes and had the motivation to win, but we had more than that. We had knowledge on how to compete. We had a winning strategy. We knew how to beat teams bigger and faster than we were. This is what we mean by intelligence. It is one of the fundamental i's that separate good teams from great teams.

W. Edwards Deming, the grandfather of Total Quality Management, once said, "Hard work and best efforts put forth without guidance of profound knowledge may well be the root of our ruination. There is no substitute for knowledge." We have witnessed the profundity of this comment time and time again. Developing effective and efficient methods for gaining knowledge and intelligence are critical to any successful enterprise. Data collection is not enough. We have to turn the data into information and the information into knowledge. Collecting data without meaningful purpose is a waste of time and talent. Organizations that are data-rich and information-poor get in their own way. Great organizations are knowledgeable. They perform with intelligence, wisdom, and awareness. They use this **i** in team to outsmart the competition.

AT A GLANCE

- Intelligence means knowing how to achieve your goals.
- Intelligence is what gives a team clear direction without unnecessary risk.
- Great team leaders use intelligence to direct their teams wisely.

TEAM EXERCISE

One of the most effective tools for building intelligence is the AAR, the After Action Review. This simple tool allows a team to conduct a post-experience review of what worked and what did not work during the experience. Athletic teams might refer to this as a post-game review where the team watches game films for the purpose of improvement. A typical AAR requires that the team review what it planned to do, what it actually did, what worked well, and what did not work well. We then complete the AAR with adjustments or action items to exercise moving forward. We like to do fifteen- to twenty-minute AARs after every team event we experience.

intu

ition

The intuitive mind is a sacred gift and the rational mind is a faithful servant. We have created a society that honors the servant and has forgotten the gift.

—Albert Einstein

Turning facts and data into useful information cannot be done without intuition. We have to exercise the right side of our brain to optimize the value of the left side. We have to ask "Why?" in addition to "Who, What, Where, How, and When?" This combination of gifts is what leads us to "aha" moments. It is what helps us connect the dots.

Intuition is what gives context to the content and keeps teams from getting trapped in trivial weeds. It is what distinguishes mental intellect from emotional intelligence. It is what breeds wisdom. We use intuition to see patterns, read between the lines, and link tactics with strategy. High-performing teams exercise intuition to adjust quickly to unplanned events and unexpected circumstances. We cannot anticipate everything and we can never have all of the facts. At some point, we have to trust our instincts and go with our gut. This gut-feel is a form of intuitive guidance. It is a gift to be appreciated, respected, and shared.

High-performing teams value intuition because it gives us a significant competitive advantage. It is what enables us to explore what has not yet been explored. It is what empowers us with imagination and intelligence to manifest new discoveries. It is what inspires ingenuity. This one simple **i** links teams to all of the other significant **i**'s. It is also very difficult to copy. How does one copy Disney's imagination or Apple's innovation? Intuition is what keeps the best of the best on the leading edge, forcing others to catch up—or apply their own intuition to leap ahead.

When we start to see problems as opportunities in disguise, we know we are exercising our intuition. They are one and the same. Is the glass really half-empty? It might depend on what's in it! When we are truly grateful for the challenges we face because we see them as solutions waiting to be discovered, we can be thankful for our intuition. When we experience sudden flashes of insight or life-changing shifts in perception, we are witnessing the power of intuition. Great teams do not deny this extraordinary form of power by resisting ideas that come from outside the box. Instead, they suspend disbelief and critical judgment and allow the creative process to enlighten the team.

Analysis and discernment will play an important part later in the problem-solving process. Early on it is important to unite the team, not divide it. We do this by exploring the current-state facts and data without criticism and defensiveness. We continue uniting and aligning the team by brainstorming possibilities and options without judgment.

Never ignore a gut feeling, but never believe that it's enough. —Robert Heller

Only when we have a thorough understanding of where we are, where we want to go, why it is important, and multiple options for how we can get there, do we weigh in with logical analysis and planning. Intuition plays a key role in this process, particularly in the creative visioning and brainstorming steps. It is intuition that leads to ingenuity.

AT A GLANCE

- Intuition is our "sixth sense."
- Intuition is our ability to think creatively, to see the big picture.
- Intuition links tactics with strategy.
- Great team leaders use intuition to focus on what really matters.

TEAM EXERCISE

Give your team a brainteaser to play with and challenge intuition. Here is an example:

In the following line of letters, cross out six letters so that the remaining letters, without altering their sequence, will spell a familiar English word:

BSAINXLEATNTEARS

Note: Few people will solve this exercise, if any. It illustrates the power of perception, assumption, and paradigms (mental boxes or thinking patterns). To solve it, one must look at the instructions a different way. An alternative interpretation of the instructions is to cross out the letters S, I, X, L, E, T, T, E, R, S, leaving the word "BANANA" remaining.

inge

nuity

I have not failed.
I've just found 1,000 ways that won't work.

—Thomas Edison

Few teams can say they have a genius *on* the team. Many more can say they experience the genius *of* the team. We witness this difference a lot. Great discoveries come from highly intuitive teams, all searching for meaning and connection between discrete data points. These teams recognize and appreciate the genius of the word *and*, meaning they see past *either-or* conflicts. Rather than approach problems with a divisive, competitive, win-lose mentality, we seek the wisdom and ingenuity of working synergistically.

When faced with an impasse between option A versus option B, for example, we look for the brilliance in both ideas and elevate to a higher level of thinking. This might be option C, D, or Z. With imagination and intuition, we trust one another to find a way that unites us, not divides us. Voting is not teamwork.

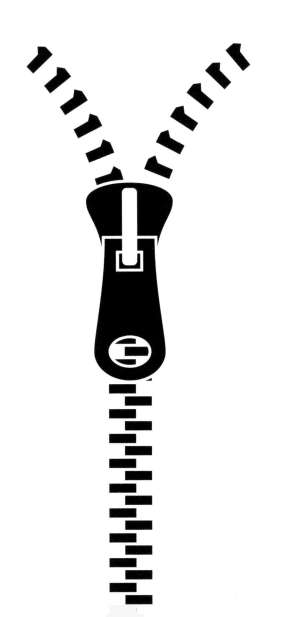

Ingenuity comes alive when we suspend disbelief and withhold judgment. The mind, like an umbrella, is more effective when it is open. To tap the ingenuity of the team, we have to accept that no one alone has all the data or all the answers. We have to listen to one another. We have to share our ideas and insights and build on them. We have to speak up and be honest with one another, even if this feels uncomfortable. We have to put the team first. Diversity and difference is a good thing. It helps us open the mind and look at things differently. Wise teams honor and respect this candid exchange of perspectives, even if it causes tension. A healthy amount of tension keeps us in balance.

In one of our workshops on teamwork, we offer a case study that I (John) developed called *The Labor Negotiations Case*. This is a true case where a management team and a labor union team could not agree on a contract. They had been bargaining for weeks, but were now at an impasse. It was clearly option A versus option B. In the exercise, we ask workshop participants to imagine they are brought in as consultants to facilitate a win-win solution. What do they do? How do they apply ingenuity to help the negotiation team see outside the box? An interesting observation with this case is that hidden beneath the conflicting "positions," both parties have common interests. They both want the same thing!

They just have different ways to get there. They are both assuming that their way is the best way—without any data to back it up! As it turns out, a combination of option A and B resolved the conflict within twenty-four hours and all parties were pleased.

Albert Einstein once said, "Any intelligent fool can make things bigger and more complex; it takes a touch of genius and a lot of courage to move in the opposite direction." Consider the wisdom in this comment the next time you are struggling with a team problem. Is the solution you are considering adding to the complexity or stripping it away? Are you trapped in the box of option A versus B? Ingenuity aims at simplifying the complex, not complicating the simple. Tap the genius of the team to awaken to alternatives. Look for option C. Chances are you have the same basic interests as the team. Use these interests to build "we-opic" vision.

AT A GLANCE

- Ingenuity is available to all of us. It does not take an individual genius.
- Ingenuity can be tapped and cultivated through teamwork.
- Great team leaders foster ingenuity by listening, empathizing, and trusting the team.

TEAM EXERCISE

Give your team a conflict-resolution exercise, like *The Labor Negotiations Case*, to allow them to work through a creative problem-solving situation. Have team members first try resolving the problem independently to collect, share, and evaluate alternatives. Then have team members break into smaller sub-teams to identify a recommended solution. Discuss and evaluate the different approaches for win-win impact. Transition the simulation to an actual example from the team. What parallels exist? How can your team apply ingenuity to current challenges?

indiv

iduals

I often warn people: Somewhere along the way, someone is going to tell you, 'There's no i in team.' What you should tell them is, 'Maybe not. But there is an i in independence, individuality, and integrity.'

—George Carlin

Make no mistake, the individuals on your team matter. Each member must bring a unique set of talents and gifts, offerings to be valued and put to good use. Each participant must bring perspective and experience, heart, mind, and soul. We all must bring something to contribute to strengthen the team. And if not, we should not be on this team! High-performing teams do not carry dead weight.

Many team leaders struggle with the "cutting edge" of high-performance teams. Indeed, this edge can be very sharp! It is what challenges us to start on time, finish on time, and manage our time well. It is what keeps us alert and accountable. It is what keeps us playing as one, in harmony and rhythm.

There is nothing soft about great teamwork. Team meetings are not friendly get-togethers where no one wants to hurt one another's feelings. These are highly disciplined events staged to accomplish something meaningful and important. Being friendly and cheerful are very positive attributes and there is certainly wisdom in providing positive reinforcement to one another, but achieving peak levels of performance requires more than this. Cheerleaders and fans can make an emotional difference, but if we have a team of unprepared, incompetent, incapable players looking to one another to hold them up, we have a recipe for disaster.

Choose the individuals for your team carefully. Make sure they bring something unique and valuable to the team. Make sure their values align with the values of the team. Diversity and differences are important, and must be respected, but values and principles must be aligned. Clarify your team expectations regarding time management, project management, ownership, discipline, visibility, and accountability. High-performing teams honor these critical success factors. We must start on time. We must come prepared. We must take ownership and step up to meet our commitments. We must put our personal differences aside and unite as a team.

We must be accountable for our actions and complete our assignments as planned. Managing our own behavior in line with team expectations and principles is a demonstration of respect. It is where we integrate the **i** in individual with the **i**'s of inspiration, interdependence, intelligence, intuition, and ingenuity. The **i** in individual is an enabler to great teamwork. It is essential to the team. If you doubt this, try building a team without it.

Take time to get to know the individuals on your team. What does teamwork mean to them? What unique gifts or talents do they have to offer? What kinds of things annoy them? What is their personality type? What kinds of things do they like and dislike? If they could offer one change to improve things, what would it be? Why?

AT A GLANCE

- Individuals matter to the team. Everyone has something to offer.
- Individuals make things interesting.
- Without individuals, there can be no team.
- Great team leaders understand, position, and align individuals to strengthen the team.

TEAM EXERCISE

Offer your team members an opportunity to use a well-researched, practical personality profile to gain more understanding about themselves, one another, and their approach to problem-solving, time management, and conflict resolution. We like to use the Myers-Briggs Type Indicator (MBTI), one of the most widely used instruments in the world. Combine this exercise with other team exercises to draw parallels between personality differences and behavioral preferences. This might be one of the most enlightening exercises you ever do.

A B C D E

A team is the sum of its individual members.

F G H I J

While selecting and nurturing qualified characters

K L M N O

is important, if you put them in the wrong positions,

P Q R S T

you will redefine your team.

U V W X Y Z

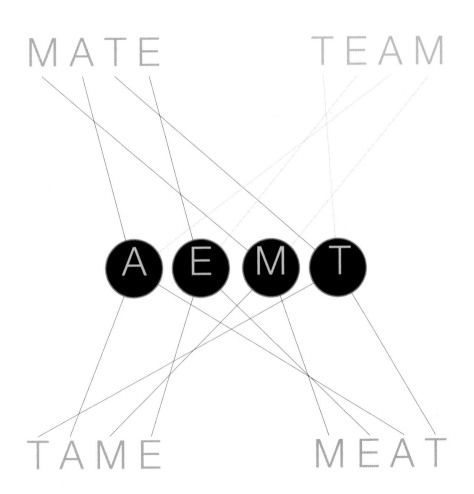

inter

action

Humankind has not woven the web of life. We are but one thread within it. Whatever we do to the web, we do to ourselves. All things are bound together. All things connect.

—Chief Seattle

Teamwork is about sharing. It requires that we speak up and offer our ideas, experiences, talents, and concerns. It also requires that we listen to one another, making sure we have a good connection. It does us little good to all talk at once with no one listening or to sit in silence, fearing embarrassment or reprimand.

Healthy teams have healthy connections. We learn to read one another. We build empathy and understanding. We look out for one another. We support one another. We cover for one another when need be. We learn to trust one another. We find ways to make each other look good. All of this requires healthy interaction.

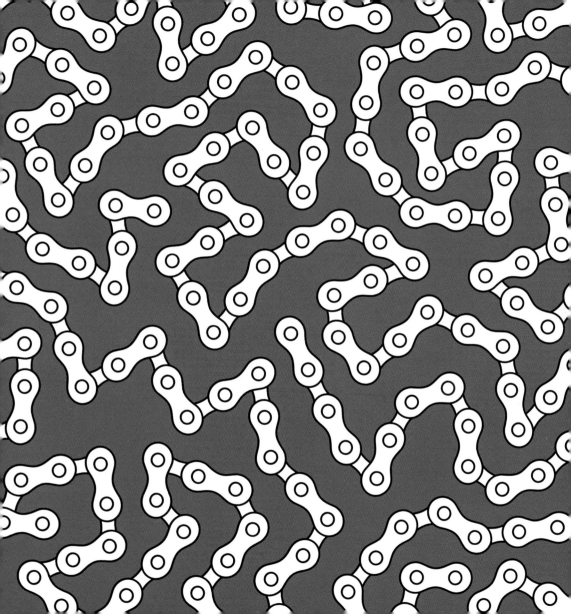

Fear, insecurity, and judgment are great inhibitors to healthy interaction. If team members are afraid, they may not speak up or share honest feedback. We must learn to suspend judgment—a form of dualistic, right-wrong thinking—to capture critical inputs. Healthy teams know how to solicit the brutal facts and communicate openly without personal and premature judgment. We use discernment to evaluate and make choices, leaving judgment to a higher power. Discernment allows us to see cause-and-effect relationships between choices without becoming emotionally attached. We seek win-win interactions rather than dualistic ego responses. We know we are using discernment rather than judgment when we do not feel superior, controlling, righteous, angry, or condemning with the choices people make. We feel at peace.

High-performing teams recognize that we must unite as one to deliver synergistic results. We must interact in harmony, like a disciplined symphony orchestra or a creative jazz band. We, indeed, have different roles to play with different responsibilities attached, but it is the synergistic interaction that leads to the quality and delivery of the music. We play as one.

AARs—After Action Reviews—provide a great opportunity for team interaction. These quick, deliberate, constructive interventions are designed to deal with the brutal facts:

1. What did we plan to do?
2. What did we actually do?
3. What worked?
4. What did not work?
5. What do we need to change going forward?

The AAR is an opportunity to revisit the game plan. Did we have a winning game plan? What worked and what did not work? Did we follow the plan? Again, what worked and what did not work? Overall, what can we learn from the experience we just had? If there is learning involved, it is hard to call any loss a true failure. In a world of continuous improvement, we have to make mistakes to accelerate learning. Innovation often comes from things going wrong!

- Interaction is what connects individual team members.
- Interaction is about building trusting, respectful relationships.
- Great team leaders stimulate interaction to build healthy relationships and empower higher performance.

TEAM EXERCISE

Revisit a recent team event or experience. Conduct an AAR on that event. Customize the AAR tool to your liking and benefit. Make sure all team members participate and interact. Document the inputs on a flipchart or notepad. Commit to the suggestions and adjustments identified and build them into your next AAR. Did the adjustments work? What else needs to change? Demonstrate that you are listening to one another, seeking to understand further improvements and willing to act on the inputs offered. Next, invite different members of the team to facilitate the AARs, reinforcing this practice as a habit. Drive out fear and open up the channels of innovation and improvement.

It is possible to build teams where the team is LESS than the sum of its members. In other words, 1 + 1 < 2. Imagine building a team where members actually subtract from each other's individual performance. How can this happen? Whether it's from incompetence, fear, or both, the results adversely impact performance. It's difficult to establish teamwork when members are focused on not messing up for fear of losing their jobs. Negative environments yield negative results. Quality teams are built on positive attitudes and trust.

Performance teamwork is predicated on synergistic interaction. Synergy is a phenomena where the "whole is GREATER than the sum of its parts." 1 + 1 = 3 or more. In addition to having the right people in the right places doing the right things, high-performance teams make certain each member is clear on its objectives. They make certain team members have shared values and embrace the **i** in team. Without synergy, teams won't experience the collective compounding effect necessary for peak performance.

inno

vation

Creativity is our most powerful asset.
It always has been. It can change reality.

—Michael McMillan

Innovation is the manifestation of imagination. It is what happens when we act on our ideas, bringing our dreams into reality.
Put simply, we are innovating when we are making positive change. I (John) like to refer to this as *Zentrepreneurship*, the combination of optimistic, compassionate Zen thinking and the discipline and fortitude of undertaking risk to bring an idea to fruition. Zentrepreneurs inspire and lead innovation.

Take a look around you. We live in a world of innovation. High-performing companies are relentlessly coming out with new products and services to outpace the old.

It takes high-performing teams to do this, people working together and applying the **i**'s of teamwork. These teams are inspired to make change. They work interdependently to find win-win solutions. They apply intelligence, intuition, and ingenuity to innovate effectively. They pull together as individuals through healthy interaction to synergize as a team. We are fortunate to see the results of this every day. We see it in technology. We see it in construction. We see it in education and healthcare. We see it in distribution. And we also see the absence of it—the painful and frustrating results of organizations that have not yet uncovered these critical **i**'s in team. Results tend to speak for themselves. Pay attention to the **i**'s in team. They do make a difference.

Recently, I (John) was giving a speech based on my book *The How of Wow: Secrets Behind World Class Service*. During the talk, I purposely showcased a cell phone that was about six years old. I highlighted the fact that this little phone could be used without any wires. All I had to do was flip it open and pull up the little antenna. I could even text with it, typing certain numbers until the desired letter popped up. The audience laughed, perhaps wondering if I was serious. "Is this a joke? Does he really expect this phone to wow us? Does this phone have email capability? Does it have a GPS? Does it have a calculator? Does it have video capability?

Can it take quality photos? Can it be used as a flashlight?" The questions and comparisons continued. How could an innovation only six years old now be considered obsolete?

Innovation is game-changing. It puts everyone back to zero if they are not positioned to keep up and even raise the bar. It does a company little good today to have a Six Sigma process for an obsolete product or practice. Many companies, large and small, have learned this lesson the hard way. Customers and stakeholders continue to expect more because they are experiencing innovation every day. We are wise to apply the i's in team to lead proactively and accomplish things never done before. Cynics and skeptics do not belong on these teams. They will drain the team of "Zenergy," the positive, powerful energy required to generate synergy. Status quo thinking puts us at risk. If we are not innovating, we are falling behind.

AT A GLANCE

- Innovation is the expression of inspiration.
- Innovation has come to be expected.
- Innovation is required to "wow" people.
- Without proactive innovation, teams are at risk.

TEAM EXERCISE

Pull your team together for a brainstorming session. Ask the team what one change could potentially put the team at serious risk. What could go wrong? How serious is this? How likely is it? What paradigm shift could send us all back to zero? Share some examples to provoke out-of-the-box thinking. Consider book and video downloads, alternative energy sources, and online banking, travel, education, and information possibilities. We have smart phones. Why don't we have smart windows, smart houses, smart glasses, smart clothes, smart vehicles, and smart traffic signals? See what your team comes up with. Use this i in team to stay in the game.

infor

mation

Ignorance, the absence of information and knowledge,
is the root cause to most of our problems. We simply do
not know what we do not know.

—John Murphy

One of our favorite team-building and leadership development exercises involves blindfolding participants and then instructing them to build a specific model out of Tinker Toys. In the first round, they are allowed only "negative" feedback by their partner, serving as a supervisor. This management approach is referred to as "management by exception." The blindfolded player is expected to do a good job, so the only feedback offered is when things go wrong.

In a second round, the supervisor is allowed to offer positive feedback. However, in both scenarios the blindfolded players are not able to reproduce the exact model in the short time allowed. The absence of important information is truly disempowering.

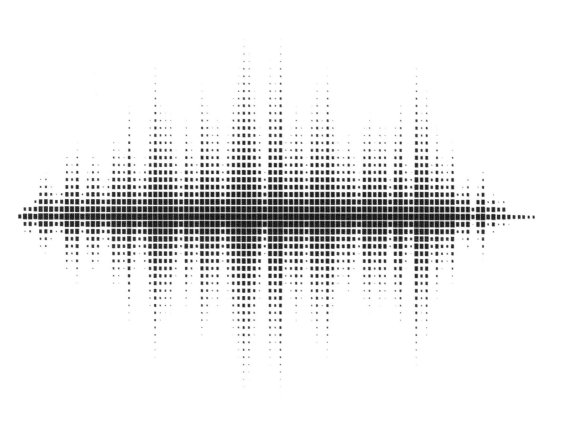

In the blindfolded exercise, we remove critical information from view. The blindfolded participants cannot see the goal and they have very limited feedback on how they are actually doing. In round one, this feedback is only negative, making the situation even worse. Without important information, people can feel helpless, frustrated, and disempowered. Without information, people are forced to assume. Without information, people cannot take responsibility effectively. Without information, people have little choice but to delegate problems *up*—to the boss!

Stop and ask yourself, how clear is your team on what is expected every day? Do they know how they are doing throughout the day, without needing to ask anyone? Are the specific goals for the day clear? Are the targets and metrics clearly understood and visible? Do team members have access to the scoreboard? Are team members positioned and enabled to take responsibility and be accountable? Have the obstacles that disempower people been removed?

Ignorance, the absence of information and knowledge, is the root cause to most of our problems. We simply do not know what we do not know. This causes us to assume, often assuming the worst.

Without information, we tend to play it safe. We want to protect ourselves. We do not want to take unnecessary risks. Ironically, we live in the information age without critical information. We have a lot of data, trivia, and drama at our fingertips, but this does not translate into crucial intelligence and knowledge.

At the end of the day, there are relatively few things we really need to know. High-performing teams use pertinent information to sharpen team focus, align resources, manage time, and execute with minimal distraction. This information includes mission-critical targets, expectations, standards, timing, and metrics.

Is your team clear on exactly what it needs to do and when?

AT A GLANCE

- Information is critical to team success.
- Information must focus the team on what really matters.
- Information must be timely, specific, and visible.
- Information must be used to gain knowledge and intelligence.

TEAM EXERCISE

Take a look at your team scoreboard. Do you have one? Does it include what the team really needs to account for behavior and results day-to-day? Is it visible? Is it user-friendly? Do you use it daily to manage effectively? Is the data collected being analyzed for further improvement opportunities? Is the information helping you gain knowledge and intelligence as a team? Pull your team together to discuss this and evaluate the current state. What changes can you suggest to improve your team's information? Where do team members feel "in the dark" and what can be done to illuminate the situation?

inte

grity

*Doing the right thing
doesn't take courage—
it takes intellectual honesty
and personal integrity.*

—Robert Owen Carr

Every i mentioned in this book is important to a team in one way or another. Every i provides a key ingredient, a key input to success. However, none may be as important as integrity. Trust is the bedrock of true high-performance teamwork. It is what gives us a solid foundation on which to build.

Strong teams require strong foundations. Things will go wrong from time to time. We won't always get the outcomes we desire. Pressure will present itself. Tension will arise. How will we respond to these challenges? Will we pat one another on the back and accept it as a lesson learned? Will we evaluate the situation objectively in our AAR, making adjustments as need be? Will we support one another? Will we continue to trust one another?

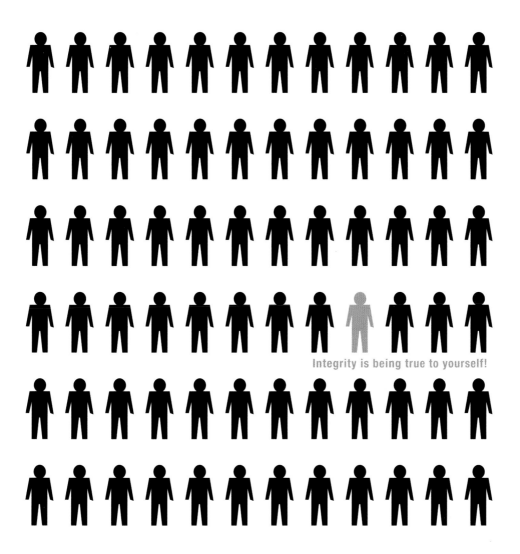

Integrity is being true to yourself!

Great teams are integrated teams—seamless, holistic, balanced, and complete. Team members are open and honest with one another. There is a collective consciousness and a state of flow, equanimity, and grace—as if team members can read one another. Think of this like exceptional dance partners, extraordinary surgical teams, or great quarterback-receiver combinations. We anticipate one another's needs and do what we can to build a stronger connection. We speak candidly and truthfully. We attack problems, not one another. We get the facts, rather than jump to conclusions. We challenge assumptions, beginning with our own. We look for and recognize the value in one another. We treat each other with respect. We walk our own talk. This may not come easily, but it allows us to know each other at a deeper level, to trust one another soul-to-soul. We commit to one another from the heart, not just the head. There is passion and compassion, all evolving from this one essential **i**.

If a man's associates find him guilty of being phony, if they find that he lacks forthright integrity, he will fail. His teachings and actions must square with each other. The first great need, therefore, is integrity and high purpose. —Dwight D. Eisenhower

Accountability is an important element of integrity and high-performance teamwork. Great team leaders demonstrate this by holding people accountable. Great teams demonstrate this by accepting accountability and holding one another accountable. How do we do this?

We set goals. We clarify expectations. We keep score. We share our values and intentions. We walk our talk. We admit our mistakes. We take corrective action. We get back up after we fall. We try again. We help one another. We cooperate. We work as one. We call this integrity. It is the bond that holds us together, defining our genuine character. It is ours for the choosing, an i for all i's and an essential i in team.

AT A GLANCE

- Integrity breeds trust, the bedrock of healthy relationships.
- Integrity defines character from the inside out.
- Integrity sets us free; there is no hiding from the truth.
- Integrity unites us, giving us authentic power and strength.

TEAM EXERCISE

Revisit your mission statement and guiding principles. If you do not have one, write one. Clarify your team mission, vision, and values. What are your guiding principles, your constants in times of change? What defines you as a team? This is your "talk." Next, examine your "walk" in relation to your talk. Do your policies, procedures, designs, work flows, metrics, systems, and structure reinforce these words? Is your organization aligned?
Are people rewarded for adhering to your principles? Is teamwork designed into your culture? Is it rewarded? Is key information shared and used for empowerment? What is missing? What investments do you need to make?

influ

ence

Everyone here has the sense that right now is one of those moments when we are influencing the future.

—Steve Jobs

While some individuals hold more sway than others, it's the members' collective influence on each other that establishes the team's character and its performance. Leaders and team members don't always recognize the impact their words and actions have on others. In truth, we are always influencing and being influenced. As it relates to teamwork, an individual's influence on team members trumps his or her title or position. Leaders can forget this point or minimize its importance. It's not uncommon to mistakenly believe we can choose which words or actions will influence others and which ones won't. Wise leaders remain cognizant that all of our words and actions matter. Simply put, we are continuously influencing others and others are continuously influencing us.

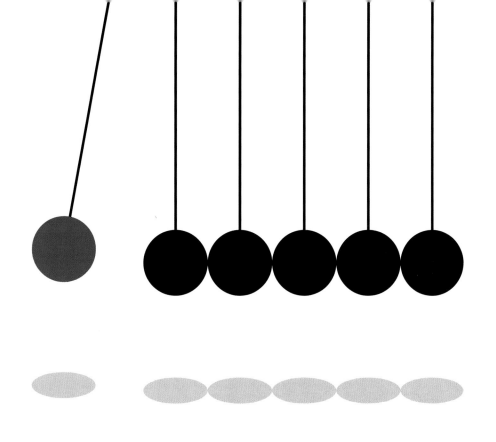

As adults, it's easy to observe many of the influences that impact children. Positive or negative, some influences have an immediate impact, while others are expressed more subtly through a person's emotions, opinions, and behaviors.

Suppose a dynamic leader is put in charge of the team. He or she can have an immediate influence. Whether or not the influence is positive, productive, or lasting is another question. Since performance teams strive for constant improvement, quality leaders focus on consistent behaviors that encourage members to do the same. These collective actions influence team performance at every level.

Think twice before you speak, because your words and influence will plant the seed of either success or failure in the mind of another. —Napoleon Hill

While everyone is influenced, some individuals are more susceptible to certain types of influences than others. For example, peer pressure has a major impact on some people's behavior. While personal integrity should prevent members from falling prey to negative peer pressure, wise leaders remain cognizant of the team's pulse and its influences.

Performance teams are guided by shared values. Individuals who don't embrace them shouldn't be on the team. This is especially true for leaders and managers. When leadership doesn't live the team's values, it undermines the team.

Imagine if your team members' attitudes were contagious viruses. Whose attitudes would you want the team to catch? Why? Whose attitude wouldn't you want them to catch? Is your attitude worth catching? Good, bad, or indifferent, attitudes can spread quickly and influence your team.

Consider your team's existing ecosystem. Is it conducive for positive-attitude viruses to dwell, prosper, and spread? What about the negative viruses? Are they being nurtured or suppressed? When a team loses a negative influencer or two, the impact on the other team members can be significant. Wise leaders create the right conditions for a positive attitude pandemic.

TEAM EXERCISE

Select a topic to which everyone on your team can easily contribute. Pick a team member to share his/her opinion on the topic. Before people can share their opinions, they must summarize the previous person's views. If they forget, or can't provide an accurate summary, they lose their chance to speak until another person finishes speaking. Monitor the conversation closely and encourage everyone to participate. Once team members grasp the concept, change the subject, and move to the next round.

In this round, those who don't or can't summarize can no longer participate in the discussion. When you reach two members, stop and discuss what you've learned about listening and influence.

inves

tment

*Optimism is a strategy for making a better future.
Because unless you believe that the future can be better, you are
unlikely to step up and take responsibility for making it so.*

—Noam Chomsky

Great leaders think in terms of ROI, return on *investment.* We know that what we sow is what we reap. We understand that nothing ventured translates into nothing gained. Risk brings reward, one way or another. Healthy teams require ongoing investment. We must fuel the team with the essential inputs to experience desired outputs.

These investments can take many forms:

- Useful and accurate information and intelligence systems
- Relevant benchmarking opportunities—best practices
- Continuous training and education
- Quality equipment, tools, software, systems, and supplies
- Meaningful incentives and rewards
- Effective leadership, mentoring, and coaching

These investments require time, presence, discipline, and money. Cultivating high-performance teamwork is like growing a garden. We get out of it what we put into it. We have to till the soil. We have to remove the obstacles. We have to pull the weeds. We have to sow the seeds. We have to provide support and nurture the process. The flowers want to blossom and the crop is meant to be harvested, but we have to help it along. We have to invest in the process. We have to pull it all together.

The i's in this book are like seeds. They must be honored, respected, planted, and nurtured to take root and grow. They may not be visible at first, and there may be doubt along the way, but make no mistake—the i's in team are vital. These seeds matter. These sacred truths give us the means to harvest great results. They represent the individuals, the ideas, and the imagination necessary for any team to prosper. They give us something to work with, something to build from. Just imagine the world without this investment.

If we open a quarrel between the past and the present, we shall find that we have lost the future. —Winston Churchill

There is an i in team. Indeed, there are many i's in team. Pay close attention. Look for the hidden truth in what may not be so obvious to the masses. Read between the lines. Challenge the boundaries of the box. Take the time and make the investment. Give your team the lift it deserves.

The future depends on what you do today. —Mahatma Gandhi

The world prospers when people pull together and challenge the status quo. We are meant to grow and work together. We are meant to flow and celebrate together. Use these i's to open eyes. The problems we face don't look so daunting when we see them though the i's of teamwork.

TEAM EXERCISE

Take a good look at your team development budget. If you do not have one, create one. Start with team selection, training, and governance. What does the team need to elevate to the next level of performance? Does it have proper guidance, coaching, and mentoring? Have you identified global best practices and benchmarks? Is your team properly trained? Does the team have effective tools and information systems? Are knowledge management systems in place? Revisit the i's in team. Identify the i's the team needs further development in. Be specific. Then add this i—make the investment!

John J. Murphy is an award-winning author, speaker, and management consultant. Drawing on a diverse collection of team experiences as a corporate manager, consultant, and collegiate quarterback, John has appeared on more than four hundred radio and television stations and his work has been featured in more than fifty newspapers nationwide.

John specializes in creating high-performance team environments, teaching leadership and team development, and leading global kaizen events. He has trained thousands of "change agents" from more than fifty countries and helped some of the world's leading organizations design and implement positive change.

John is a critically acclaimed author and sought-after speaker. Among his other books are: *Zentrepreneur: Get Out of the Way and Lead—Create a Culture of Innovation and Fearlessness*; *Pulling Together: 10 Rules for High Performance Teams*; *Beyond Doubt: Four Steps to Inner Peace*; *Reinvent Yourself: A Lesson in Personal Leadership*; *Agent of Change: Leading a Cultural Revolution*; *Sage Leadership: Awakening the Spirit in Work*; *The Eight Disciplines: An Enticing Look Into Your Personality*; *Habits Die Hard: 10 Steps to Building Successful Habits*; *Leading with Passion: 10 Essentials for Inspiring Others*; and *The How of Wow: Secrets to World Class Service*.

Portrait by: Janice Foerch

John J. Murphy

Founder and president of Venture Management Consultants

venturemanagementconsultants.com

Michael McMillan

michaelmcmillan.com

Michael McMillan is an internationally renowned designer, bestselling author, creative consultant, and highly regarded public speaker. His breadth of knowledge and experience, combined with his unique insight and story-telling ability, make him a much-sought-after speaker. Michael speaks to audiences around the world on a number of topics. His presentations are original, fresh, and honest; he connects with audiences of all ages, leaving them both motivated and committed to embrace a future of endless possibilities.

Early in his career, Michael founded a visual communication firm that, according to a major publication, "attracted a client roster that read like the *Who's Who of Business.*" In addition to his strategic branding and marketing communication work, Michael's creative direction on Michael Jordan's *New York Times* bestselling pictorial autobiography, *Rare Air,* established a new niche in retail publishing. He followed this success with several award-winning coffee-table books including *Mario Andretti, The NBA at 50,* and John Deere's *Genuine Value.*

A critically acclaimed author, Michael's other books include *Pink Bat: Turning Problems Into Solutions; The Power of Teamwork;* and *Paper Airplane: A Lesson for Flying Outside the Box.*

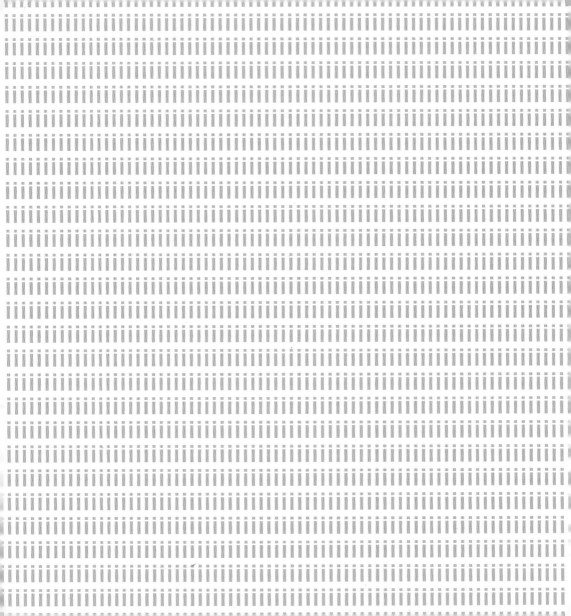